W9-BNE-161

SELENA GOMEZ

Kayleen Reusser

Mitchell Lane
PUBLISHERS

P.O. Box 196
Hockessin, Delaware 19707
Visit us on the web: www.mitchelllane.com
Comments? email us: mitchelllane@mitchelllane.com

PUBLISHERS

Printing   1   2   3   4   5   6   7   8   9

A Robbie Reader
Contemporary Biography

Abigail Breslin	Albert Pujols	Alex Rodriguez
Aly and AJ	Amanda Bynes	Ashley Tisdale
Brenda Song	Brittany Murphy	Charles Schulz
Dakota Fanning	Dale Earnhardt Jr.	David Archuleta
Demi Lovato	Donovan McNabb	Drake Bell & Josh Peck
Dr. Seuss	Dwayne "The Rock" Johnson	Dylan & Cole Sprouse
Eli Manning	Emily Osment	Hilary Duff
Jaden Smith	Jamie Lynn Spears	Jesse McCartney
Jimmie Johnson	Johnny Gruelle	Jonas Brothers
Jordin Sparks	LeBron James	Mia Hamm
Miley Cyrus	Miranda Cosgrove	Raven-Symoné
Selena Gomez	Shaquille O'Neal	Story of Harley-Davidson
Syd Hoff	Tiki Barber	Tom Brady
Tony Hawk		

Library of Congress Cataloging-in-Publication Data
Reusser, Kayleen.
  Selena Gomez / by Kayleen Reusser.
     p. cm. — (A Robbie reader)
  Includes bibliographical references and index.
  ISBN 978-1-58415-752-6 (library bound)
  1. Gomez, Selena, 1992– —Juvenile literature. 2. Actors—United States—Biography—Juvenile literature. 3. Singers—United States—Biography—Juvenile literature. I. Title.
  PN2287.G585T54 2009b
  791.4302'8092—dc22
  [B]
                                                                2009004531

ABOUT THE AUTHOR: Kayleen Reusser has been interviewed on radio, TV, and in print. She has written several children's books, including *Taylor Swift* for Mitchell Lane Publishers. She has also published thousands of articles in newspapers, magazines, and books, including the Chicken Soup series. Reusser lives in Indiana and is a member of Toastmasters, an organization that improves public speaking. Find out more about Reusser at www.KayleenR.com.

PUBLISHER'S NOTE: The following story has been thoroughly researched and to the best of our knowledge represents a true story. While every possible effort has been made to ensure accuracy, the publisher will not assume liability for damages caused by inaccuracies in the data, and makes no warranty on the accuracy of the information contained herein. This story has not been authorized or endorsed by Selena Gomez.

TABLE OF CONTENTS

Words in **bold** type can be found in the glossary.

Selena Gomez and Demi Lovato have been friends since meeting on the set of the popular children's program *Barney & Friends*. Since then, both actresses have starred in movies. Their production of *The Demi and Selena Show* can be seen on YouTube.

Audition for *Barney*

Selena Gomez didn't think about the people watching her from behind the camera. She forgot about the hundreds of other children waiting to **audition** (aw-DIH-shun) as a child actor on the program *Barney & Friends*. Instead, she focused on singing, dancing, and smiling.

Selena, seven, and her mother had driven to Dallas, Texas, from their nearby home in Grand Prairie, Texas, for the audition. "I want to be an actress," Selena had told her mother. Trying out for a part on *Barney & Friends*, she believed, would help her reach that goal.

One thousand four hundred children showed up for the audition. At the end of the day, the people who produced the show chose Selena for the part!

Selena played the character of Gianna on *Barney & Friends* for two years. Being on the show helped her learn stage directions, camera angles, and good manners. "Saying 'please' and 'thank you' became a habit," she told the *Contra Costa Times* several years later.

By age six, Selena knew she wanted to be an actress. With hard work and determination over the decade since then, she has established herself as one of Hollywood's busiest actresses.

Her experience on Barney helped Selena earn a role in the 2003 movie *Spy Kids 3-D: Game Over.* Though she had a small part as the Waterpark Girl, Selena got to meet such famous actors as Antonio Banderas, Tony Shalhoub, Salma Hayek, George Clooney, and Emily Osment.

Selena's talent attracted the attention of people at the Disney Channel. When Selena was twelve, they asked her to star in two new TV programs. Unfortunately, the shows never made it on the air.

Selena didn't let these disappointments discourage her. She continued to act, appearing in commercials for T.G.I. Fridays and Chili's restaurants. She also appeared on TV shows such as *The Suite Life of Zack & Cody* and *Walker, Texas Ranger.* In the movie *Brain Zapped*, Selena had the lead role of a girl who investigates strange happenings in a library. She also sang the theme song for *Brain Zapped.*

All of this work kept Selena busy. Still, she hoped for a steady acting job.

Demi Lovato, Miley Cyrus, and Selena have helped each other become successful entertainers. Selena's role on *Hannah Montana* gave her acting experience, which led to a starring role in *Wizards of Waverly Place*.

Going to California

Finally, in 2007, Selena landed a guest role as the nasty pop star Mikayla on the popular Miley Cyrus show *Hannah Montana.* Selena hoped someday to have her own show like Miley. She didn't know it, but her dream was about to come true.

The officials at the Disney channel again contacted Selena. "We'd like you to be in a new TV **sitcom**," they told her. "You'll have two parents, and an older and a younger brother." That sounded good to Selena, an only child.

On *Wizards of Waverly Place,* Selena's character, Alex Russo, and her brothers, played by actors Jake T. Austin (Max) and David Henrie (Justin), perform acts of magic that get them into and out of trouble.

Selena had a request for the show's writers. "I don't want to wear heels," she said. "Please have Alex wear Converse shoes." Selena, who likes to dress in a T-shirt and jeans, has over twenty pairs of Converse shoes in her closet at home.

When Selena is not acting, she enjoys hobbies like cooking, photography, going to movies, and playing video games with friends and family.

During summer breaks when not filming *Wizards of Waverly Place*, Selena and the rest of the cast, including Jake T. Austin (top), Jennifer Stone, and David Henrie, call each other often to stay in touch.

When *Wizards of Waverly Place* **premiered** (preh-MEERD) on the Disney Channel in October 2007, an estimated 5.9 million people watched it. That made *Wizards of Waverly Place* the top-rated TV series that night on cable!

Selena and country music star Taylor Swift have each recorded albums and music videos. Friends now, they support each other's careers. Taylor congratulated Selena at the premiere of *Another Cinderella Story*.

The success of *Wizards of Waverly Place* brought other acting jobs to Selena. She provided her voice for the character of the Mayor's daughter in the movie *Horton Hears a Who!* She also had the lead role in the romantic musical film *Another Cinderella Story.* Andrew Seeley, the movie's male lead actor, had performed in the *High School Musical* concert tour.

The first film was so popular, a **sequel** to *Another Cinderella Story* was scheduled to be released in 2009, as was a movie based on *Wizards of Waverly Place.* Selena starred in both. She also appeared in the Jonas Brothers' video *Burnin' Up.*

Meanwhile, she continued to sing. She crooned the tune "Fly to Your Heart" for the movie *Tinker Bell.* Selena's **rendition** (ren-DIH-shun) of the song "Cruella de Vil" was included on *101 Dalmatians—2 Disc Platinum Edition.*

Selena Gomez has become one of the busiest and most popular actors in America. But life has not been easy.

Selena credits her family, including her mother, Mandy and step-father, Brian Teefy, for teaching her how to balance acting with life.

Growing Up in Texas

Selena Gomez was born on July 22, 1992, in New York City. Her parents, Mandy Cornett and Ricardo Gomez, named their daughter after a famous Latina singer, Selena Quintanilla Perez.

Mandy had an Italian background, while Ricardo came from a Hispanic family in New Mexico. They divorced when Selena was five years old. Money was scarce, so Mandy, who was sixteen years old when Selena was born, took her daughter to Grand Prairie, Texas, to be closer to family. Finances improved when Selena began earning money for her acting jobs.

Mandy knew that **celebrities** (seh-LEB-rih-teez) sometimes make poor choices as a way to escape the constant pressure from

15

fans to perform and look good. Before Selena and Mandy moved to Los Angeles, California, where Selena would begin working on *Wizards*, Mandy talked to her daughter.

"You're going to hear the word yes a lot in California," Mandy told Selena. "So I'm going to tell you no on some things. I love who you are now and I don't want you to change." It wasn't

Although Selena prefers hanging out in jeans, a T-shirt and Converse athletic shoes, she also likes dresses and attending fashion shows.

that she didn't want her daughter to grow up. She wanted to keep her out of trouble.

Selena trusts her mother to help her. "Mom is with me everywhere I go," she told *Girls' Life* in 2008. "Sometimes on the set, I just need to see her face. I'm like, 'Mom, I need to see you.'"

At home Selena is treated like any other kid. "Mom makes me do my own laundry, help out with the dishes, and clean my room," she told *Contra Costa Times* in 2008.

Like many child actors, Selena is homeschooled. Sometimes it can be tricky to juggle acting with studying. On her blog for May 7, 2008, she wrote, "Today was the first table read (rehearsal when the actors sit around a table and read lines together) for season 2 of *Wizards*. The table read went great and then I was off to school. I have a book report that I am a little bit behind on, so I have to do school work, plus catch up on the book report, UGGHH!!!!"

Selena loves watching sports, including soccer. She roots for the
Kansas City soccer team called the Wizards.

Family and Friends

Selena doesn't work all the time. She enjoys sports, especially basketball (she's a big fan of the San Antonio Spurs), cooking, photography, rock and roll music, and all things British. "I want to go to London so bad," she says.

But there is one place Selena prefers above all others: home. "I go home—at least, I try to—once a month," she told *Girls' Life*. "I'm really close to all my family—cousins, aunts, grandmother, and grandpa. I've had the same friends since kindergarten. It was definitely hard to leave them."

Selena misses other things from Texas. "I like eating pickles while watching a movie," she says. "They don't sell pickles in theaters in L.A."

One thing Selena did not have to leave behind was her best friend, Demi Lovato.

"Demi and I met when we did *Barney* together," said Selena. Demi played a character named Angela. They also acted together in the 2009 movie *Princess Protection Program*. And in 2008, the two started a show on YouTube called *The Demi and Selena Show.*

Selena is thankful for Demi's friendship throughout the years. "We're going through the madness together," she told Maggie Rodriguez on *The Early Show* in October 2008. "I'm so blessed and happy she's there because you meet a lot of people you may not be able to trust."

In the same interview, Selena said she knows some people look to her and Demi as role models for other young people. "I'm glad my job is to be a role model. But we're sixteen-year-olds. We're going to make mistakes. I'm trying to make mistakes only to myself and not my fans."

Selena donates much of her time to helping others, including children at A Time for Heroes Celebrity Carnival, sponsored by the Elizabeth Glaser Pediatric AIDS Foundation.

Hoping to make the right choices in deciding what movies to appear in, Selena formed her own movie company, July Moon Productions, in 2008. She was also planning to release her first album with Hollywood Records in the summer of 2009.

By staying focused on her goals of being an actress, Selena Gomez has earned the recognition of children across America. She was voted Favorite TV Actress at the Nickelodeon Kids' Choice Awards in March 2009.

Leading the Cause

Celebrities like Selena are sometimes asked to promote charities or special events. A few months before the 2008 United States presidential election, Selena served as the national **spokesperson** for UR Votes Count.

At dozens of shopping malls around the country, a UR Votes Count display was set up where teens could learn about **candidates** (KAN-dih-dayts) running for president of the United States. They could then cast their votes in a **mock** election.

Selena, sixteen, believed it was important for teens to know what the candidates planned to do if elected president. Even though they are too young to vote, teens should be informed on issues such as the environment and education. (A U.S. citizen must be eighteen years old to vote). "These issues affect us all," she told *Women's Wear Daily* in August 2008. "In a few years, we'll be ready for one of our greatest responsibilities—voting."

Also in 2008, Selena served as the national Trick-or-Treat **ambassador** (am-BAS-uh-der) for UNICEF (the United Nations

In October 2008, Selena became the youngest UNICEF Trick-or-Treat ambassador in the organization's 58-year history. She encouraged children to collect money for charity. "This is one way kids can help other kids in need," she said.

As the star of a popular Disney show, Selena is well known to children throughout the United States. At the St. Jude Children's Hospital's 5th annual Runway for Life Benefit, she mingled with some of her young fans.

Selena has worked most of her life to earn her dream of being an entertainer. From films and TV to recording albums and creating programs on the Internet, Selena has proven she is willing and able to tackle any project.

Children's Fund, formerly known as the United Nations International Children's Emergency Fund).

As ambassador, Selena encouraged children to ask for money instead of candy at Halloween. The money would be used to buy food and medicine for poor children around the world. Selena told *Entertainment News,* "I want to help encourage other kids to make a difference in the world and show them that 'Trick-or-Treat for UNICEF' is such a great, fun way to get involved."

One thing Selena has always done, no matter what project she's been involved with, is be herself. "I was never the girl who needed to make sure I looked like all the other girls," she wrote on her Facebook page. "I think you look best when you stand out."

She offers the same advice to young people. "Be yourself always," she says. "There's no one better!"

CHRONOLOGY

1992 Selena Gomez is born in New York City on July 22.

1999 Selena lands the role of Gianna, a child on *Barney & Friends*, which she'll keep for two years.

2003 She appears as the Waterpark Girl in the movie *Spy Kids 3-D: Game Over.*

2005 She appears in an episode of *Walker, Texas Ranger.*

2006 Selena stars as Emily Grace Garcia in *Brain Zapped.* She sings the theme song for the movie.

2007 She appears as Mikayla in several episodes of *Hannah Montana.* She leads the cast of *Wizards of Waverly Place*, which premieres on the Disney Channel in October. Selena sings the theme song for the show.

2008 Selena provides her voice as the Mayor's daughter for *Horton Hears a Who!* She has the lead role as Mary in *Another Cinderella Story* and sings several songs for the sound track. Selena forms her own movie company, July Moon Productions. She appears in the Jonas Brothers' video *Burnin' Up.* She sings tunes for the movies *Tinker Bell* and *101 Dalmatians–2 Disc Platinum Edition.* Selena signs a record deal with Hollywood Records to release her first album in summer 2009.

2009 Disney premieres *Princess Protection Program.* Selena wins a Nickelodeon Kids' Choice Award for Favorite TV Actress. A film based on *Wizards of Waverly Place* is to be released. A sequel to *Another Cinderella Story* is to be released. She stars in the film *Ramona and Beezus*, based on the book by Beverly Cleary.

FILMOGRAPHY

2009 *Princess Protection Program*

2008 *Another Cinderella Story*

     Horton Hears a Who! (voice)

     Appearance in Jonas Brothers' video, *Burnin' Up*

2007 *Wizards of Waverly Place* (TV)

2006 *Brain Zapped*

2003 *Spy Kids 3-D: Game Over*

1999–2001 *Barney and Friends* (TV)

DISCOGRAPHY

Albums

2009 *Selena Gomez* (tentative title)

Sound Track Contributions

2008 *Tinker Bell*–"Fly to Your Heart"

     101 Dalmatians–2 Disc Platinum Edition "Cruella de Vil"

     Another Cinderella Story–"New Classic," "Tell Me Something I Don't Know," "Bang a Drum"

FIND OUT MORE

Books

Perelman, Helen. *Wizards of Waverly Place #1: It's All Relative!* New York: Disney Press, 2008.

Ryals, Lexi. *Best Friends Forever: Selena Gomez & Demi Lovato.* New York: Price Stern Sloan, 2008.

Tieck, Sarah. *Selena Gomez.* Edina, Minnesota: Buddy Books, 2009.

Tracy, Kathleen. *Demi Lovato.* Hockessin, Delaware: Mitchell Lane Publishers, 2010.

FIND OUT MORE

Works Consulted

Barney, Chuck. " 'Wizards' Star's Magical Mix of Charm, Talent." *Contra Costa Times* (Walnut Creek, CA), February 7, 2008.

Campbell, Janis. "Meet Selena Gomez, Wizard in Training." *Detroit Free Press*, October 18, 2007.

Girls' Life. "What's Hot." September 2008, p. 45.

Moin, David. "General Growth Properties Stages Mock Election for Teens." *Women's Wear Daily*, August 19, 2008, Vol. 196, Issue 37.

Philpot, Robert. "Charmed Lives: With the New Supernatural-themed 'Wizards of Waverly Place,' Two North Texas Teens Get Their Big Break . . ." *Fort-Worth Star-Telegram* (TX), October 12, 2007.

Rizzo, Monica. "Meet TV's New Tween Stars." *People*, October 22, 2007.

"Selena Gomez Named UNICEF Spokeswoman." *Entertainment News*, October 9, 2008.
http://www.upi.com/Entertainment_News/2008/10/09/Selena_Gomez_named_UNICEF_spokeswoman/UPI-31331223568240/

"Selena Gomez: Proud of Start on *Barney*." *The Early Show*, October 23, 2008. http://www.cbsnews.com/stories/2008/10/23/earlyshow/main4541439.shtml

Siegel, Tatiana. "Gomez Forms Production Arm." *Daily Variety*, October 30, 2008.

Tan, Michelle, and Lisa Ingrassia. "Is Selena Gomez . . . the Next Miley Cyrus?" *People*, May 26, 2008.

White, Kelly. "Feelin' the Love Selena Gomez." *Girls' Life*, February 2008.

On the Internet

Disney: Wizards of Waverly Place
http://tv.disney.go.com/disneychannel/wizardsofwaverlyplace/

Facebook: Selena Gomez
http://www.facebook.com/pages/California-City-CA/Selena-Marie-Gomez/45011916891

Myspace: Official Selena Gomez Page
http://www.myspace.com/selenagomez

Selena Gomez: Official Site
http://www.selenagomez.com/

YouTube: Official Selena Gomez page
http://www.youtube.com/selenagomez

GLOSSARY

ambassador (am-BAS-uh-der)—A person who represents a large group or cause.

audition (aw-DIH-shun)—A tryout for a movie, play, or other performance.

candidate (KAN-di-dayt)—A person who seeks an office, honor, etc.

celebrity (seh-LEB-rih-tee)—A famous person.

mock (MOK)—Imitation.

premiere (preh-MEER)—A first public performance or showing of a play or film.

production (proh-DUK-shun)—A presentation for the stage, screen, radio, or television.

rendition (ren-DIH-shun)—A personalized version, as of a role or a piece of music.

sequel (SEE-kwul)—A story that follows the action and characters of another story.

sitcom (SIT-kom)—Short for "situation comedy," a funny show about people in a certain situation, such as being wizards in a fancy neighborhood.

spokesperson (SPOHKS-per-sun)—Someone who speaks for another person or for a group.

PHOTO CREDITS: Cover, pp. 1, 3, 26—Jason Merritt/FilmMagic/Getty Images; p. 4—Jean-Paul Aussenard/Wirelmage/Getty Images; p. 6—Todd Anderson/Walt Disney World via Getty Images; p. 8—K. Mazur/TCA 2008/Wirelmage/Getty Images; p. 10 Jason LaVeris/Wirelmage/Getty Images; p. 11—AP Photo/Disney Chanel, Bob D'Amico; p. 12—Todd Williamson/Wirelmage/Getty Images; p. 14—Mathew Imaging/Wirelmage/Getty Images; p. 16 Michael Tran/FilmMagic/Getty Images; p. 18—Scott Pribyl/MLS via Getty Images; pp. 21, 22—Mark Sullivan/Wirelmage/Getty Images; p. 24—Brian Ach/Wirelmage/Getty Images; p. 25—Stefanie Keenan/Wirelmage/Getty Images. Every effort has been made to locate all copyright holders of material used in this book. If any errors or omissions have occurred, corrections will be made in future editions of this book.

INDEX